# NEW YORK TRAVEL WRITERS SOCIETY
*A professional society for travel writers and photographers*

# ANNUAL REPORT

## FY 2013

*New York Travel Writers Society Annual Report including financial statement, and, 2014 By-Laws including updates and amendments*

# 2013

## Contents

## A Letter to New York Travel Writers Society Members

## March, 2014

Dear NYTWS Members,

The time for me to step down as your Chairwoman has come, and, a number of factors played a part in this difficult decision. Having been forced to make a choice between NYTWS or my business and personal life, I must choose my business and personal life over continuing to act as Chairwoman of the group. This does not mean the group is dissolving, and, I am pleased to announce that reorganization is currently in process, and, I will be serving the group in an advisory capacity behind the scenes.

At this time, Mike Dunphy will serve as the new Chair (or more precisely group leader) as changes to New York Travel Writers Society begin in March, 2014. Changes include corporate structure, organization name, and, additions to the Board of Directors. I ask that you be patient and give Mike Dunphy and the new ideas (along with the new members he is bringing aboard) a chance to succeed. He has wonderful visions for the future of NYTWS, and, with your support he will flourish and create an even stronger organization for all members.

It has been an honor and privilege to have been your Chairwoman with so many well respected members in the hospitality media industry among us. I can only I hope I served the group well, and, more importantly that I have remained true to Sofia Braganza's vision for the organization as she had originally planned prior to her untimely passing.

I wish you all continued success with your careers, and, hope that one day our paths will cross again.

Most sincerely,

T.R. "Tina" Threston

## TIMELINE

The following represents amendments that have been implemented by the Board of Directors and also demonstrates financial amendments to New York Travel Writers Society.

### June, 2011

Sofia Braganza, Founder, creates New York Travel Writers Society and sends out invitations to join.

### June, 2012

New York Travel Writers Society joins LinkedIn and a Board of Directors is formed. Sofia Braganza is Chairwoman.

## June, 2013

- Founder and Chairwoman Sofia Braganza passes away
- T.R. "Tina" offers Chair position to entire BOD before accepting position
- T.R. "Tina" Threston moves into position as Chairwoman

## March, 2014

- T.R. "Tina" Threston steps down as Chairwoman after a total of 2.5 years serviced as Chairwoman and Vice-Chairwoman of NYTWS.
- Mike Dunphy was nominated and confirmed by the BOD to be interim Chairman as restructuring of the organization takes place.
- T.R. "Tina" Threston donates 50% of her share of Luxury Travel and Lifestyles Magazine to NYTWS to help the organization generate revenue.
- New York Travel Writers Society Board of Directors begin restructuring process including corporate structure and name.

- Voting on amendments to the By-Laws including creation of an Honorary Advisory Board of Directors. All amendments pass with majority vote March 4, 2014 and implemented March 5, 2014

- March 6, 2014 current BOD renames New York Travel Writers Society to New York Travel Media Society. Purchases domains and begin paperwork for group.

# Financial Summary

## New York Travel Writers Society Expense Report

## 2012 – 2014

*Unless otherwise noted all expenses were paid by T.R. Threston (including the time Sofia Braganza was Chairwoman. Reimbursement was never paid for these expenses). The limited amount of money coming in from paid memberships was used to help off-set T.R. Threston's expenses.*

| Operating Expenses | Monthly | Yearly | Two Year Total |
|---|---|---|---|
| Virtual Office – 375 Park Ave, NY NY | $170 per month | $2040 | $4080 |
| Website with Hosting | $50 per month | $600 | $1200 |
| Business Email | $12.50 per month | $150 | $300 |
| TOTAL | $232.50 per month | $2790 per year | $5580 two year total |

## Start Up Costs and Miscellaneous Expenses

## 2012 – 2014

*Unless otherwise noted all expenses were paid by T.R. Threston (even during the time Sofia Braganza was Chairwoman. Reimbursement was never paid for these expenses.) The limited amount of money coming in from paid memberships was used to help off-set T.R. Threston's expenses.*

Name domains.

- NYTWS.org
- NYTWS.com

Trademark.

Trademark Process $99 + $325 USA government filing fees = $424

Press Releases.

A package was never purchased for NYTWS for press releases, instead, an "as needed" method was applied. The average cost of the press releases are $100 per release.

- New York Travel Writers Society 2013 Awards (May 7, 2013; SBWire.com)
- New York Travel Writers Society Announces 2013 Travel Award Winners (May 16, 2013; SBWire.com)
- New York Travel Writers Society announces 2013 Award nominations are now open for businesses (March 4, 2013; onlineprnews.com)

## 2013 TWA AND NYTWS Award Expenses

*Unless otherwise noted all expenses were/are being paid by T.R. Threston (even during the time Sofia Braganza was Chairwoman. Reimbursement was never paid for these expenses.) The limited amount of money coming in from paid memberships was used to help off-set T.R. Threston's expenses. TWA is a dissolved professional group which NYTWS partially absorbed and $5000 was given to NYTWS towards expenses of awards purchasing and distribution.*

**$12,879.00 - $5000 (from TWA) = $7879**

## 2012 - 2014 Charitable Fundraising/Giving

| Charity | Amount Raised 2012 | Amount Raised 2013 | Amount Raised 2014 (To Date) | Number of NYTWS Members Participating |
|---|---|---|---|---|
| KIVA* | $0.00 | $3400 | $525 | 11 |
| CAMBOBABS | $0.00 | $0.00 | $0.00 | 0 |
| Haiti Education Foundation | $0.00 | $0.00 | $0.00 | 0 |
| The Muskoka Foundation: Do Good As You Go | $0.00 | $0.00 | $0.00 | 0 |

*The NYTWS KIVA Team was dissolved in February, 2014 due to the lack of participation. Members who did participate have joined T.R. Threston's personal KIVA which has raised $12,275 (as of March 4, 2014) since it's inception in 2012.

# New York Travel Writers Society Income Generated

## 2012 – 2014

As of March 4, 2014 registered members on the NYTWS.org website totaled 239. Of 239 members the following were paid membership and represent the only income generated by New York Travel Writers Society from inception to March 4, 2014.

## Membership Levels and Definitions

ANNUAL REGULAR MEDIA MEMBERSHIP (New Applicant and Lapsed Member) - $175.00 (USD) Subscription period: 1 year No recurring payments For new applicants and past members with lapsed membership status.

ANNUAL REGULAR MEDIA MEMBERSHIP (Renew) - $150.00 (USD) Subscription period: 1 year No recurring payments For current members in good standing only. All other applicants please select ANNUAL REGULAR MEDIA MEMBERSHIP (New Applicant and Lapsed Member)

ASSOCIATE MEMBERSHIP (LODGING, PR FIRM, TOURISM OFFICE, ETC.) - $225.00 (USD) Subscription period: 1 year No recurring payments For new applicants and lapsed members

ASSOCIATE MEMBERSHIP (LODGING, PR FIRM, TOURISM OFFICE, ETC.) - Renew - $200.00 (USD) Subscription period: 1 year No recurring payments For current members in good standing only

NON PROFESSIONAL MEMBERSHIP (New applicants and Lapsed Members) - $50.00 (USD) Subscription period: 1 year No recurring payments For new applicants and lapsed members

NON PROFESSIONAL MEMBERSHIP (Renew) - $25.00 (USD) Subscription period: 1 year No recurring payments For current members in good standing only

SUPPORTING and STUDENT MEMBERSHIPS (New Applicant and Lapsed Member) - $100.00 (USD) Subscription period: 1 year No recurring payments New Applicants and Lapsed Members

SUPPORTING and STUDENT MEMBERSHIPS (Renew) - $75.00 (USD) Subscription period: 1 year No recurring payments For current members in good standing only

TWA Membership Special - $120.00 (USD) Subscription period: 1 year No recurring payments You must have been a member of Travel Writers Association prior to May 1, 2013. This offer expires August 31, 2013. Member rate of $120 is only valid the first year.

**Charter Membership\*\***

*Special Note: Of 239 members registered on NYTWS.org 230 members fall into Charter Membership and only five renewed as paying members in 2013/2014*

Free one-year charter membership is available to all LinkedIn group members and to all new members coming in from TWA until April 30, 2013.

Paid members transferring from TWA may apply their TWA membership dues as credit against a paid NYTWS membership.

Benefits:

- Personal profile page on the NYTWS website
- Eligible for Press Trips & Press Card
- Eligible to submit articles for consideration NYTWS magazine (print & online) (exclusive to NYTWS members only)
- NYTWS newsletter with valuable member information
- Receive regular email announcements and be eligible to apply for NYTWS member press trips
- Annual NYTWS conference
- Professional development workshops at conference
- Eligibility to be a Regional Membership Representative for your geographical area
- NYTWS awards events (discounted entry fees for members)
- Post your articles (links) on the NYTWS website.
- Display your photographs in the photo gallery of the NYTWS website

At the end of one year, charter members may choose to apply for any applicable NYTWS membership category.

Membership and Income Generated through March, 2014 – Total $1750 from inception to 04/04/2014

| Membership Level | Membership Dues | Number of NYTWS Members Participating | Number of Registered Lapsed Memberships | Total Income Generated by Membership 2012 - 2013 | Total Income Generated 2013 -2014 |
|---|---|---|---|---|---|
| Annual Media Membership | $175 | 6 | 6 | $1050.00 | $0.00 |
| Annual Media Membership (Renewal) | $150 | 0 | 3 pending renewal not processed | $0.00 | $0.00 |
| Associate Membership | $225.00 | 2 | 2 | $450.00 | $0.00 |
| Associate Membership (Renewal) | $200.00 | 0 | 1 pending renewal not processed | $0.00 | $0.00 |
| Non Professional Membership | $50 | 1 | 1 | $50.00 | $0.00 |
| Non Professional Membership (Renewal) | $25 | 0 | 0 | $0.00 | $0.00 |
| Supporting and Student Memberships | $100 | 2 | 2 | $200 | $0.00 |
| Supporting and Student Memberships (Renewal) | $75 | 0 | 0 | $0.00 | $0.00 |
| TWA Special Rate | $120 | 3 | 3 | 0 | $0.00 |
| Charter Membership | Free | 225 | 225 | $1750.00 | $0.00 |

# FOUNDING MEMBERS, BOARD OF DIRECTORS AND CONTRIBUTORS

**Prepared & Approved for Publication by the 2013/2014 Board of Directors**

- T.R. "Tina" Threston - Chairwoman
- Susan Carter – Vice Chairwoman
- Richard Montuori - Director of Media Relations
- Maria Liberati - Director of Public Relations; Spokesperson
- Amaka Nwigwe – Board Member
- Bryan Pereira – Board Member
- Mike Dunphy – Board Member

**Founding Members**

- Sofia Braganza
- T.R. "Tina" Threston
- Susan Carter
- Richard Montuori
- Maria Liberati
- Amaka Nwigwe
- Bryan Pereira
- Mike Dunphy

**Contributors to NYTWS Launch in 2012/2013 (in addition to the Founding Members above)**

Contributors are recognized as helping the organization launch, and, at one point were Board of Director members, but, who served less than one full year on the BOD.

- John Lamkin
- Heidi Fuller Love
- Michael McDermott

# Contact Information

New York Travel Writers Society

Website: http://nytws.org

NEW YORK TRAVEL WRITERS SOCIETY
*A professional society for travel writers and photographers*

New York Travel Writers Society 2013 Bylaws

With 2014 Amendments

Updated March 6, 2014

## Amendments 2012/2013/2014

In total 12 amendments were passed on March 3, 2014 by NYTWS Board of Directors. The amendments are available for inspection during regular business hours along with the voting results. Contact the Board of Directors for further of information. The new Honorary Advsiory Board of Directors mission statement and by-laws are included at the end of this report.

# New York Travel Writers Society

# Board of Directors as of 02/27/2014

- T.R. "Tina" Threston - Chairwoman
- Susan Carter – Vice Chairwoman
- Richard Montuori - Director of Media Relations
- Maria Liberati - Director of Public Relations; Spokesperson
- Amaka Nwigwe – Board Member
- Bryan Pereira – Board Member
- Mike Dunphy – Board Member

Mike Dunphy was confirmed as the interim Chairman as restructuring of NYTWS begins in March, 2014. The new BOD and corporate structure beginning March 1, 2014 will be updated at a date no later than January 30, 2015.

ARTICLES

## ARTICLE I. PURPOSE

1.01. This Corporation is organized under New York Nonprofit Corporation Law. Specific purposes of this Corporation are as follows:

1. Provide a central meeting point and resource base for active members. Members include both professional and non-professional individuals in the fields of food, wine, travel, and hospitality related businesses,
2. Provide knowledge and information to the general public regarding food, wine, travel, and hospitality,
3. Create and maintain a high standard of professional ethics and recognize achievements of members through Awards on an annual basis,
4. Provide professional growth opportunities by providing seminars, conferences, workshops, professional development courses within the food, wine, travel and hospitality industries for our members,
5. Create and maintain a scholarship program for young adults who wish to enter the food, wine, travel and hospitality industries,
6. Contribute and fundraise for other related nonprofit organizations including, but not limited to *The Kids Cooking Network*.

## ARTICLE II.OFFICES

2.01. The principal headquarters of New York Travel Writers Society is located at 375 Park Avenue, New York, NY 10152. The Board of Directors has the power and authority to change its location and add additional offices as deemed necessary. Any such changes will be noted in the Bylaws but will not be considered an amendment.

## ARTICLE III. BOARD OF DIRECTORS as of June, 2013

3.01. The Board of Directors shall consist of no more than **11Directors** including the chairperson. The following are the 2013 Founders and Board of Directors and their respective titles:

- **Sofia Braganza**, CEO, Chairperson & Treasurer
- **T.R. (Tina) Threston**, 1st Vice Chair; Co-Treasurer; Deputy Editor-in-Chief, ETA magazine; Director Events Committee; Chair Press Trips Committee

- **Susan Frost**, 2$^{nd}$ Vice Chair, Co-Treasurer; Deputy Press Officer; Chair Publicity Committee, Co-Chair Membership Committee

- **S. Mar Carter**, Secretary; Co-Treasurer; Editor-in-Chief, ETA magazine
- **John Lamkin**, Director of Global Membership; Chair;Membership Committee
- **Richard Montuori**, Director of Media Relations
- **Maria Liberati,** Director of Public Relations; Spokesperson
- **Heidi Fuller-Love**, Director of Committees; European Press Officer
- **Michael McDermott**, Director of Charity Affairs

**3.02 Order of Succession.** The following is the status of each titled position with Chairperson ranking highest and most important and Director of Charity Affairs as the least important. This ranking system is only for the Order of Succession, and, it has no impact on voting power or other status of the New York Travel Writers Society Board of Directors.

1   Chairperson
2   1$^{st}$ Vice-Chair
3   2$^{nd}$ Vice-Chair
4   Secretary
5   Global Director of Membership
6   Director of Media Relations
7   Director of Public Relations
8   Director of Committees
9   Director of Charity Affairs

If there are more than eight Board members, a vote may be enabled to determine the next order of succession.

The Board of Directors cannot be dismissed or replaced in the event a new chairperson takes over. All Board of Directors members serve in their position for a period of two years. At that time the BOD member has the option of renewing their status or stepping down.

**3.03 Board of Directors Attendance.** Each member of the New York Travel Writers Society Board of Directors of Directors is required to attend at least 40 percent of all events and functions sponsored by New York Travel Writers Society with two exceptions where 100 percent is required. BOD members must attend the annual Holiday Gala and Awards Ceremony and BOD members must attend the annual meeting.

**Only the following will exempt BOD members from these two commitments:**

- Call to Duty (including military, police, firefighters, and, other indispensable public safety members)
- Death or serious illness with you or with in your immediate family (including in-laws and also in cases of civil unions or long term relationships)
- Highly contagious, infectious illness such as flu
- Urgent primary job related issues (this will be decided on a case by case basis)

If the reason for missing either the Holiday Gala and Awards Ceremony or BOD annual meeting is not listed above, the reason for absence may be presented to the BOD members. If the BOD deems the absence unreasonable then the BOD member in question may be asked to step down from his or her position. In the case of a tie, the chairperson makes the final decision.

### ARTICLE IV. MEMBERS

### Classification and Qualification of Members

4.01. New York Travel Writers Society shall have six classes of members, as follows: Board of Directors Member, Charter Member, Member, Blogger/Non-Professional Member, Student Member, and, LinkedIn Member. All but Blogger/Non-Professional Members, Student Members, and LinkedIn Members shall have the right to vote when voting is enabled.

Section 4 of these Bylaws also deems that Blogger/Non-Professional Members, Student Members, and, LinkedIn Members are not eligible for office or becoming members of the New York Travel Writers Society Board of Directors of Directors, nor are they eligible for Press Trips.. In all other respects, the rights, and interests of each member, regardless of classification in New York Travel Writers Society are equal, except as stated in this Section.

### Eligibility for Membership

3.02. The following persons are qualified to be members of New York Travel Writers Society:

3.02.1. Any person over age 21 is qualified for any category of membership in the

Corporation, except for student members who must be over the age of 18.

3.02.2. A candidate for Board of Directors, Charter, Member, Blogger/Non-Professional, Student and LinkedIn membership in New York Travel Writers Society should have an interest and/or broad experience and/or background in the industries, as previously described, with a desire to uphold ethical standards set by New York Travel Writers Society as well as an interest in professional growth and networking within the industries outlined.

3.02.3. Regular members are required have **their original work published for at least 12months prior to membership and continuously during membership.** Said work should have been

presented in public media, including, but not limited to, newspaper, magazines such as restaurant and/or travel or hospitality trade publications, radio, television, internet, and, compensation must have been received for the work. Regular members are hereby said to be "professionals" and may be referred to as professional members.

Fees and Dues

3.03. Fees and dues shall be payable from time to time as fixed by the New York Travel Writers Society Board of Directors.

3.03.1. The Directors are authorized to fix an amount for dues from time to time and make them

payable at such time, times, or intervals, and on such notice as they may prescribe or deem as necessary.

3.03.2. Memberships shall be non-assessable and non-refundable.

Corporate Records

3.04. New York Travel Writers Society shall keep adequate records of account and written minutes of the proceedings of its Board, members and committees. New York Travel Writers Society is also required to publish a financial statement each year and the statement is due within 45 days of filing its annual tax return.

New York Travel Writers Society is also required to keep a current membership list, including the name and means of contact such as address, phone, fax or electronic mail address, and, class of each member.

Termination of the membership of any member shall be recorded in the membership list, along with the date such membership ceased. All such records shall be available for inspection by the members, and shall be written or in a form capable of being converted into written form.

**Inspection Rights of Membership**

3.05 Subject to New York Travel Writers Society's right to set aside a demand for inspection pursuant to Article 6 of the New York Corporations Code and the power of the court to limit inspection rights pursuant to § 607 of the New York Corporations Code, and unless a Corporation provides a reasonable alternative as permitted by these Bylaws, a member satisfying the qualifications set forth hereinafter may do either or both of the following:

> a. Inspect and copy the record of all the members' names, addresses, and voting rights, at reasonable times, on five business days prior written demand on New York Travel Writers Society, which demand shall state the purpose for which the inspection rights are requested; or

> b. Obtain from the Secretary of New York Travel Writers Society, on written demand and tender of a reasonable charge, a list of the names, addresses, and voting rights of those members entitled to vote for the election of Directors, as of the most recent record date for which it has been compiled or as of the date of demand. The demand shall state the purpose for which the list is requested. The membership list shall be available on or before the later of 10 business days after the demand is received or after the date specified therein as the date as of which the list is to be compiled.

3.05.1. The rights of inspection set forth in Section 3.05 of New York Travel Writers Society Bylaws may be exercised by the following:

> a) Any member, for a purpose reasonably related to such person's interest as a member; and b),The authorized number of members for a purpose reasonably related to the members' interest as members.

3.05.2. New York Travel Writers Society may, within 10 business days after receiving a demand pursuant to Section 3.05 of these Bylaws, deliver to the person or persons making the demand, a written **offerfrom the New** York Travel Writers Society of an alternative method of achieving the purpose identified in said demand without providing access to or a copy of the membership list. An alternative method which reasonably and in a timely manner accomplishes the proper purpose set forth in a demand made pursuant to Section 3.05 of New York Travel Writers Society Bylaws shall be deemed reasonable, unless within a reasonable time afteracceptance of the offer, New York Travel Writers Society fails to do those things which it offered to do. Any rejection of the offer shall be in writing and shall indicate the reasons the alternative proposed by New York Travel Writers Society does not meet the proper purpose of the demand made pursuant to Section 3.05 of these Bylaws.

**Non-liability of Members**

3.06. A member of New York Travel Writers Society shall not solely, because of such membership, be personally liable for debts, liabilities, or obligations of New York Travel Writers Society.

**Termination of Membership**

3.07. The termination of membership in New York Travel Writers Society will be affected by the following:

3.07.1. Membership of any member of New York Travel Writers Society shall automatically terminate (a), on the member's written request for such termination delivered to a member of the New York Travel Writers Society Board of Directors personally, by facsimile, electronic mail, or by United States mail, or (b),upon the member's death.

3.08.2. Membership of any member who fails to pay dues when they become due, andsubsequent to the delinquent date set therefore, shall automatically terminate provided thatwritten notice is given to the member personally communicating such dues were due andpayable, or by United States mail, or by facsimile, or electronic mail within 10 days before the due date specified hereinabove. In the event that such written notices is not given as herein required, then such membership shall automatically terminate for nonpayment of dues, only if they are not fully paid within 30 days after such written notice is eventually given and delivered to the member in person, by facsimile, electronic mail, or deposited in the United States mail, postage prepaid, and sent to the member's address as it appears on the records of New York Travel Writers Society.

3.07.3. All rights of the member shall cease on termination of membership as herein provided, orupon suspension or expulsion pursuant to Section 3.08. If any document of membership has been issued, it shall be returned to New York Travel Writers Society for cancellation. Any member upon termination shall immediately cease the use of any business cards, stationery or any other document which represents him to be a member of New York Travel Writers Society.

3.07.4. Any member terminated under this Section may re-apply and be readmitted by meeting

the requirements of Section 3.03.

**Suspension and Expulsion of Members**

3.08 A member of New York Travel Writers Society in any category may be fined, suspended or expelled for cause by majority vote of the New York Travel Writers Society Board of Directors, pursuant to the following procedure:

1. The Board, or a designated committee, shall notify the member in writing of the charge(s) or basis for action.

2. The member shall have 30 days to submit documents to rebut the allegations. Upon request, and for good cause, the New York Travel Writers Society Board of Directors may allow the member such additional time as is reasonably necessary to gather and submit evidence.

3. The member may request to appear in person, by teleconference, on online chat conference, before the New York Travel Writers Society Board of Directors to rebut the allegations, including the right to bring supporting witnesses.

4. If no appearance is requested, or if the member does not appear, the New York Travel Writers Society Board of Directors shall vote, based on the existing evidence and the report of whoever conducted any investigation.

5. If the member appears, the New York Travel Writers Society Board of Directors shall conduct an informal hearing, to receive any relevant information offered. The Board may vote at that time, take the matter under advisement, or extend the time for receipt of evidence, as it deems warranted.

6. The Board shall promptly notify the member in writing of its decision. A fine, suspension or expulsion shall be effective immediately upon receipt by the member of the New York Travel Writers Society Board of Directors' decision.

3.08.1. A suspension may be complete or partial, or for any period of time the New York Travel Writers Society Board of Directors deems appropriate for the violation(s) committed. An expulsion shall render the member ineligible for readmission for at least two years following the effective date of the expulsion.

3.08.2. "Cause," as used herein, includes the failure of the member to abide by the Articles of

Incorporation, Bylaws or Code of Professional Conduct of New York Travel Writers Society; or the commission of some act(s) prejudicial to the purpose of New York Travel Writers Society.

3.08.3. All rights of the member in New York Travel Writers Society shall cease on the member's expulsion.

**Transferability of Membership**

3.09. Neither the membership in New York Travel Writers Society nor any rights in the membership may be transferred for value or otherwise.

**ARTICLE IV. MEETINGS OF MEMBERS**

4.00. Place of Meeting of Members

4.01. Meetings of the membership shall be held at such places as may be designated from time to time by the New York Travel Writers Society Board of Directors.

**Regular and Annual Meetings**

4.02. The members shall meet annually at a time and date during the months of _____ or ___ selected by the New York Travel Writers Society Board of Directors for the purpose of transacting such business as may come before the meeting and hold elections as necessary for Board of Director vacancies every second year. If the election of Directors shall not be held at any such annual meeting or at an adjournment thereof, or if such meeting is not held, the New York Travel Writers Society Board of Directors shall cause the election to be held by written ballot sent to each voting member by the United States mail, postage prepaid, addressed to the member's address as it appears on the books of New York Travel Writers Society and returned within 20 days after each mailing. If the day fixed for the annual meeting falls on a legal holiday, such meeting shall be held at the same hour and place on the next succeeding day.

### Special Meetings

4.03. Special meetings of members shall be called by no less than three Board of Directors members of New York Travel Writers Society, or by a petition signed by no less than 30 percent of the voting members on no less than 10 days written notice to the membership, as set forth in 4.04.

### Notice of Meetings

4.04. Written notice of the time and place (and, in the case of Special Meetings, the general nature of the business to be transacted) of every meeting shall be delivered personally to each voting member by first-class mail, fax, electronic mail, or by publication in New York Travel Writers Society newsletter at least 10 days prior to said meeting. Membership addresses shall be available at the principal office of New York Travel Writers Society (375 Park Avenue, New York, NY) during regular business hours for anyone attempting to call a meeting pursuant to 4.03.

### Quorum

4.05. A quorum at any meeting of members shall consist of 50 percent of the voting power, represented in person or by proxy.

### Adjournment for Lack of Quorum

4.06. In the absence of a quorum, any meeting of the members may be adjourned from time to time by the vote of the majority of the voting members present in person or by proxy, but no other business shall be transacted except as provided in Section 4.08.

### Notice of Adjourned Meeting

4.07. When a meeting is adjourned for 30 days or more, notice of the adjourned meeting shall be given as in the case of the original meeting. When a meeting is adjourned for less than 30 days, it is not necessary to give any notice of the time and place of the adjourned meeting or of the business to be transacted thereat other than by an announcement when the adjournment is taken.

Loss of Quorum

4.08. The members present at a duly called or held meeting at which a quorum is present may continue to do business until adjourned, notwithstanding the withdrawal of enough members to leave less than a quorum, if such action taken other than adjournment, is approved by at least a majority of members required to constitute a quorum.

Voting

4.09. Voting at a meeting of members shall be conducted as follows:

4.09.1. Each member is entitled to one vote. Voting at meetings shall be by voice vote, except as otherwise expressly provided in these Bylaws. Votes may be conducted by postal mail, fax, electronic mail, or telephone.

4.09.2. No single vote may be split into fractional shares.

4.09.3 Voting members may vote by written proxy, given to any other voting member attending

the meeting in person, with a copy filed with the Secretary of New York Travel Writers Society, prior to the vote. Proxies may be general, for a term of up to eleven months, or specific for a single issue. The holder of a proxy who will not be able to attend a meeting may transfer the proxy to another voting member, with a copy of the transfer filed with the Board of Directors of New York Travel Writers Society prior to the vote. A fax, photocopy, or electronic email message shall be as valid as a signed original.

Conduct of Meetings

4.10. Meetings of members shall be presided over by the Chairperson or Vice-Chairperson. And, follow the Succession of Order as stated in section 3.02 thereafter.

Written Consents

4.11. Whenever the law, the Articles of Incorporation of this Corporation, or these Bylaws authorize members to give their written assent or consent to action of New York Travel Writers Society in lieu of attending and voting at duly held meetings, such written consents may be given by, and shall be accepted from persons who are voting members, as shown by the books of New York Travel Writers Society, at the time their consents or their proxies are given. Any member giving a written consent, or proxy, may revoke the consent prior to the time that written consents of the number required to authorize the proposed action have been filed with the Board of Directors of New York Travel Writers Society, but may not do so thereafter.

**Action Without Meeting by Written Ballot**

4.12. Any action without a meeting is authorized if by written ballot as follows:

4.12.1. Any action which may be taken at a meeting of members may be taken by ballot, subject to the following requirements:

a. The New York Travel Writers Society distributes a written ballot to every voting member, indicating the number of responses needed to meet the quorum requirement and shall state the percentage of approvals necessary to pass the measure submitted. It shall also state the time by which the ballot must be received to count;

b. Any action which may be taken at any regular or special meeting of members may be taken without a meeting provided there is satisfaction of the following ballot requirements;

c. The number of votes cast by ballot within the time period specified equals or exceeds the quorum required to be present at a meeting authorizing the action; and,

d. The number of approvals equals or exceeds the number of votes that would be required to approve at a meeting at which the total number of votes cast was the same as the number of votes cast by ballot.

**ARTICLE V. DIRECTORS**

**Number of Directors**

5.01. New York Travel Writers Society shall have no more than eleven (11) Directors, collectively known as the New York Travel Writers Society Board of Directors. The number may be changed by amendment, alteration or repeal of this Bylaw, but at no time shall the number of directors be fewer than five (5).

**Power of Directors**

5.02. The powers of the Directors shall be as follows;

5.02.1. Subject to any restrictions or limitations imposed by law, by the Articles of Incorporation, or by these Bylaws, the powers of New York Travel Writers Society are vested in the New York Travel Writers Society Board of Directors which may delegate the performance of duties and exercise of power to officers and agents of New York Travel Writers Society from time to time as it shall by resolution determine.

5.02.2. The Board of Directors shall administer the business of New York Travel Writers Society and shall have full authority to act so long as such action is not inconsistent with the Bylaws, where such action is necessary prior to the next regular meeting of the membership.

**Duties of Directors**

5.03. It shall be the duty of the Directors to:

5.03.1. Perform any and all duties imposed on them collectively or individually by law, by the Articles of Incorporation of this Corporation, or by these Bylaws.

5.03.2. Prescribe the duties and fix the compensation, if any, of all agents and employees of the

Corporation.

5.03.3. Supervise all officers, agents, and employees of New York Travel Writers Society to assure that their duties are properly performed.

5.03.4. Require that special meetings of members be called whenever and as often as they deem necessary and whenever demanded by the required number of members as in these Bylaws provided.

**Vacancies**

5.09. Vacancies on the New York Travel Writers Society Board of Directors shall exist (1), on the death, removal or resignation of any member of the Board of Directors and (2), whenever the number of Directors has authorized an increase.

5.09.1. The Board of Directors may declare vacant the office of a Director if declared of unsound

mind by an order of court, convicted of a felony, or if within sixty (60) days after notice of selection, the elected Director does not accept the office either in writing or by attending a meeting of the New York Travel Writers Society Board of Directors.

5.09.2. All vacancies shall be appointed by Order of Succession as outlined in these Bylaws OR by a majority of the remaining Directors, though less than a quorum, as hereinafter defined, or by the sole remaining Director. Any person appointed by the New York Travel Writers Society Board of Directors to fill a vacancy shall require 51 percent approval by Board of Directors members by vote or proxy.

5.09.3. If the New York Travel Writers Society Board of Directors accepts the resignation of a Director tendered to take effect at a future time, it shall appoint a successor to take office when the resignation becomes effective if the Order of Succession is not followed. To override the Order of Succession, a 51 percent approval by the Board of Directors members by vote or proxy is required.

5.09.4. A person appointed to fill a vacancy on the New York Travel Writers Society Board of Directors shall hold office for the unexpired term of the predecessor or until the Director's death, resignation, or disability as in these Bylaws provided.

**Reduction of Number**

5.10. A reduction of the number of the Board of Directors authorized shall not result in the removal of any Director prior to the expiration of the Director's term of Office.

**Compensation of Directors**

5.11. No member of the New York Travel Writers Society Board of Directors shall receive any compensation from New York Travel Writers Society, **waiver** of fees, etc. for their service on the board. Board members, however, are eligible for the same benefits as any other member.

**Meetings**

5.12. Meetings of the New York Travel Writers Society Board of Directors of Directors shall be conducted as follows:

5.12.1. Meetings shall be held in person, by teleconference, by electronic mail, or online chat conference as designated by resolution of the New York Travel Writers Society Board of Directors. Special meetings of the New York Travel Writers Society Board of Directors may be called by the Chairperson, or if absent, or unable, or refuses to act, by any Vice-Chairperson, or by any three Directors. Such meeting shall be held in person or by teleconference or by electronic mail or by online chat conference upon a minimum of 48 hours notice to all Directors by the means listed in this section.

5.12.2. Whomever calls the meeting, shall deliver written notice of the time and place of meetings to each **Directory**by mail, telephone, fax, or email at least 10 days prior to the date of the meeting, or two  days prior to Special meetings under Section 5.12.1.

5.12.3. A majority of the existing number of Directors constitutes a quorum for transaction of business.

5.12.4. Every act or decision done or made by a majority of the Board of Directors present in person or by proxy at a meeting duly held at which a quorum is present in person or by proxy is the act of the Board of Directors, unless the law, the Articles of Incorporation of this Corporation, or these Bylaws require a greater number.

5.12.5 The transactions of any meeting of the New York Travel Writers Society Board of Directors, however called or noticed, or wherever held, are as valid as though the meeting had been held under proper call and notice, provided a quorum is present and provided that either before or after the meeting each of the Directors not present signs a waiver of notice or a consent to holding the meeting or an approval of the minutes thereof. All such waivers, consents, or approvals shall be filed with the corporate records or made a part of the minutes of the meeting.

5.12.6.Except as otherwise expressly provided in these bylaws, or by law, no business shall be considered by the New York Travel Writers Society Board of Directors at any meeting at which a quorum is not present in person or by proxy, and the only motion which the chair shall entertain at such meeting is a motion to adjourn.

However, a majority of the Directors present, in person or by proxy, at such meeting may adjourn from time to time until the time is fixed for the next regular meeting of the New York Travel Writers Society Board of Directors.

5.12.7. Meetings shall be presided over by the Chairperson of New York Travel Writers Society or, if absent, by a Vice-Chairperson, or in the absence of both, by a chairman chosen by a majority of the Board of Directors present.

**Action by Unanimous Written Consent Without Meeting**

5.13. Any action required or permitted may be taken without a meeting if all members of the Board shall individually or collectively consent in writing to such action. Such action by written consent shall have the same force and effect as the unanimous vote of the New York Travel Writers Society Board of Directors. Any certificate or other document filed under any provision of law which relates to the action so taken shall state that the action was taken by unanimous written consent of the New York Travel Writers Society Board of Directors without a meeting and that the Articles of Incorporation and Bylaws of this Corporation authorize the Directors to so act and such statement shall be prima facie evidence of such authority.

Liability of Directors

5.14. The Directors shall not be personally liable for the debts, liabilities, or other obligations of

New York Travel Writers Society.

Removal of Board of Directors Members

5.15. The entire Board of Directors, or any individual Director, may be removed from office at any time by the vote of a 51 percent majority of the voting members of New York Travel Writers Society. If any or all Directors are so removed, new directors may be elected at the same meeting and they shall hold office for the remainder of the terms of the removed Directors.

**Director's Proxy**

5.16. The Board of Directors may be represented at any meeting by Proxy. The Proxy may be in any form expressing its intent; a fax, electronic email message, or photocopy shall be as valid as a signed original; Proxies may be given for all issues to be decided during that meeting, or limited to any particular issue(s).

**Indemnity by Corporation for Litigation Expenses of Officer, Director, or Employee**

5.17. Should any person be sued either alone or with others because that person is or was a Director or Officer of New York Travel Writers Society in any proceeding arising out of that person's duties or out of any alleged wrongful act against New York Travel Writers Society or by New York Travel Writers Society, indemnity for reasonable expenses, including attorneys' fees incurred in the proceeding for that person's defense, may be assessed against New York Travel Writers Society, its receiver, or its trustee, by the court in the same or a separate proceeding if (1), the person sued is successful in whole or in part, or the proceeding is settled with the approval of the court, or (2), the court finds that person's conduct fairly and equitably merits such indemnity. The amount of such indemnity shall be so much of the expenses, including attorney's fees incurred in the defense of the proceeding, as the court determines and finds to be reasonable.

**ARTICLE VII. COMMITTEES**

**Committees**

7.01. Committees for any reasonable purpose may be formed by a member of the Board of Directors.

7.02. Committees may also be formed by members and presented to the Board of Directors for approval. The petition must include:

1   The Name of the Committee
2   The Reason for Forming the Committee including how the Committee will benefit members or the Board of Directors

## ARTICLE VIII. MISCELLANEOUS

### Execution of Instruments

8.01. The Board of Directors, except as otherwise provided by these Bylaws, may by resolution

authorize any officer or agent of New York Travel Writers Society to enter into any contract or execute and deliver any instrument in the name of and on behalf of New York Travel Writers Society. Such authority may be general or confined to specific instances. Unless so authorized, no officer, agent, or employee shall have any power or authority to bind New York Travel Writers Society by any contract or any engagement, or to pledge its credit, or to render it liable pecuniary for any purpose or in any amount.

8.01.1. Except as specifically determined by resolution of the New York Travel Writers Society Board of Directors or as otherwise required by law, checks, drafts, promissory notes, notes for the payment of money, leases, contracts and other evidences of indebtedness by New York Travel Writers Society may be signed by any officer for a sum not to exceed dollars $3,000.00. Sums in excess of $3,000.00 shall be signed by any two officers.

8.01.2. All funds of New York Travel Writers Society shall be deposited from time to time to the credit of the Corporation in such banks, trust companies, or other depositories or escrow account such as PayPal as the New York Travel Writers Society Board of Directors may select.

### Corporate Seal

8.02. The Board of Directors shall adopt and use, and may at will alter, a corporate seal.

8.02.1. The seal shall be affixed to all corporate instruments, but failure to affix it shall not affect

the validity of such instrument.

**Fiscal Year**

8.03. New York Travel Writers Society shall be on a fiscal year basis. Effective Date of Bylaws:

8.04. These Bylaws shall become effective on their adoption. Amendment to these Bylaws shall become effective immediately on their adoption or at such later time as specified in the amendment.

8.04.1. Subject to the limitations contained in the Articles of Incorporation of New York Travel Writers Society and to any provisions of law applicable to these amendment of Bylaws of a nonprofit mutual benefit corporation, these Bylaws or any of them may be altered, amended, or repealed and new Bylaws adopted by a written vote of the membership. Passage requires approval by a 51 percent majority vote of those members who vote on the proposal.

8.04.2. The original or a copy of these Bylaws, as amended or otherwise altered to date and certified by the Board of Directors of New York Travel Writers Society, shall be kept in a book which shall be kept in the principal office of New York Travel Writers Society located at 375 Park Avenue, New York, NY, USA, and such book shall be open to inspection by the members at all reasonable times during office hours.

8.04.3 Within the first year after adoption of these Bylaws, the New York Travel Writers Society Board of Directors may amend them by 51 percent majority vote to correct any clerical errors or procedural defects, so long as such amendment does not alter substantive rights of the membership provided by these Bylaws.

**Annual Report**

8.06. New York Travel Writers Society shall notify each member yearly of the member's right to receive a financial report pursuant to New York Corporations Code. The annual report shall be prepared not later than 120 days after the close of the Corporation's fiscal year which ends on December 31.

New York Travel Writers Society

Honorary Advisory Board of Directors

Created and Implemented March 4, 2014

**_Mission Statement:_** To provide former Board of Directors members with rights and special privileges along with Board of Director voting rights for the lifespan of each member and the lifespan of the organization. Only former members of the Board of Directors (who stepped down in good standing and served the group for a minimum of 12 months) may be invited to join the Honorary Advisory Board of Directors. These rights cannot be revoked for any reason including but not limited to: changing of the organization name, officers, location, illness or mental incapacitation.

*The amendment to create an Honorary Advisory Board of Directors was voted upon and passed in March 4, 2014 and cannot be over tuned or revoked for any reason for the entire lifespan of the group and regardless of changes of name, charter, corporate/non-profit status or selling or merging the group with another.*

**_Membership Benefits_**

1. *Free, lifetime membership with NYTWS (or future name of the organization) at the highest membership level and includes all perks and privileges of this top membership level.*
2. **_For Board of Director Members who served 2012 – June, 2014 prior to T.R. Threston stepping down as Chairwoman only._** *The distinction of "Founding Member" along with position held will always be noted on all materials where names appear, and, a separate Founding Members section is to be added to the by-laws and on any website or printed material that represents the group privately or publicly. The members of the Founding Members group are strictly limited to:*
    a. *Sofia Braganza, Founder and Chairwoman*
    b. *T.R. Threston, Co-Founder and Chairwoman*
    c. *Susan Carter, Co-Founder and Vice Chairwoman*
    d. *Richard Montuori, Co-Founder and Director of Media Relations*
    e. *Maria Liberati, Co-Founder and Spokeswoman*
    f. *Amaka Nwigwe, Co-Founder, Board Member*
    g. *Bryan Pereira, Co-Founder, Board Member*
    h. *Mike Dunphy, Co-Founder, Board Member*

3. FREE, lifetime tickets, admission and/or permission at the highest level set for each and every Honorary Advisory Board of Directors member and one guest at any and all NYTWS (or future organization name) run functions and events.

4. Retain the first right of offering and acceptance/refusal for any and all participation in Press, Charity or other types of trips and shall be accorded the same discounting or compensated rates as all other members.

5. Each and every Honorary Advisory Board of Director members retain voting rights on the NYTWS (or future name) Board of Directors and must be included in each and every item that requires votes. Should a member of the Honorary Advisory Board of Directors fail to participate in a vote that vote defaults to the current Chairperson to enable him or her to pass or veto the item requiring the vote. Honorary Advisory Board of Directors Members have no other duties and are not responsible financially in any way for the group.

6. Honorary Advisory Board of Director members are to receive any and all "perks" that are bestowed upon the NYTWS (or future name) Board of Directors without exception this includes but is not limited to gifts, salaries, "swag bags", free travel, free advertising and all other related services and/or items.

7. The Honorary Advisory Board of Directors and the Founding Members (T.R. "Tina" Threston, Susan Carter, Richard Montuori, Maria Liberati, Amaka Nwigwe, Bryan Pereira and Mike Dunphy) are to receive a small stipend of $250 per person, per year as residual compensation for time and money spent to get the organization up and running. This stipend lasts the entire lifespan of each member of the Honorary Advisory Board of Directors.

8. Annual Meeting expenses for the Honorary Advisory Board of Director members are to be subsided by NYTWS (or future name) for half the cost. For example, if the cost to attend the organization Annual Meeting is $2,000 then NYTWS pays $1000 and Honorary Advisory Board of Director members pay $1000. All Founding Members receive ALL EXPENSES PAID special privileges for any and all Annual Meetings, and, must be notified of the event a minimum of 90 days in advance.

9. A full, and on-going updated, professional biography shall be maintained for each Honorary Advisory Board of Director and Founding Member on the Organizations website and other in all other primary media and publications as appropriate and agreed.

10. The Organization agrees to publish at least two articles and or / two photographs annually, as submitted by each Founding Member, for the life of all online and printed publications associated with the Organization. These articles and submissions will be compensated at full ongoing compensation industry rates. Additionally each Founding Member, if they so choose, will have the opportunity to annually act as an Honorary Editor for at least one edition of any publication (online or print form) of the Organization.

11. No Founding Member of the BOD is to be responsible for the debts of the organization from its inception through its expiration.

END